Sir.

Thank you for

FROM SCAR TO STAR

allowing me to
serve as one
of your Usher.
God bless you
More.

Bridgett

xulon
PRESS

DEDICATION

This book is dedicated to God the Father,
God the Son, and God the Holy Spirit. Thank You
for inspiring me all the way through to the completion
of this book.

APPRECIATION

To my king, my wonderful husband, Pastor John Israel,
for his effectual and fervent prayers and support.

To my jewel, my precious daughter, Miracle Ruth
Edison, for her sacrifice and support.

To my wonderful Grace Emenogu for typing the manuscript.

To Pastor Christy Ogbeide for her contribution toward this book. God bless you.

To my mother Martha Fominyam for encouragement and support.

To Zion leadership and its members for their continual support. I wouldn't trade you for silver or gold. You are the best. You are number one!

Contents

Hymn
HIGHER GROUND

I'm pressing on the upward way,
New heights I'm gaining every day;
Still praying as I'm onward bound,
Lord, plant my feet on higher ground.

Chorus

Lord, lift me up and let me stand,
By faith, on Heaven's tableland,
A higher plane than I have found;
Lord, plant my feet on higher ground.

My heart has no desire to stay
Where doubts arise and fears dismay;
Though some may dwell where these abound,
My prayer, my aim, is higher ground.

I want to scale the utmost height
And catch a gleam of glory bright;
But still I'll pray till Heav'n I've found,
"Lord, plant my feet on higher ground.

INTRODUCTION

I sincerely believe that every human being has a great destiny. Its manifestation is determined by how much that person strives to possess all that God has for him or her. Know today that God's plans for you are good and not evil (see Jeremiah 29:11). You did not choose the place, country, state, or nation where you were born. You did not choose your family, race, or circumtances. But your destiny is not determined by any of those external factors, but how you make good use of the time and talents that God has given you.

This book, *From Scar to Star*, is a short story of my journey in life so far. I am determined by the special grace of God to fulfill my destiny, enjoy my God-given life to the fullest, and be a blessing to others. The grace of God is always accessible as long as we acknowledge that it is only by God's mercy and goodness that we will win. All we have to do is to ask the Lord for His grace, and He will certainly answer.

I strongly believe that in these pages and with the help of Almighty God, you will be inspired to keep on trusting and serving God and to be sincerely committed to Him with all your might, soul, and body. God will continue to fight your battles and give you victory at all times and in every circumstance. In Jesus Christ, your life is headed for the best!

Chapter 1

From Scar to Star

I was born into a royal pagan family in Cameroon, Africa. I was rejected by my father because he was expecting a boy who could be the heir to the throne. When I turned out to be a girl, he announced to my mother, "Woman, I need a son—not girls. For the third time, you have had a girl. I am not sending any cloth or oil for this baby."

My grandmother, who had next to nothing except her compassionate heart, quickly took me in. Her little hut, composed of a living room, kitchen, and bedroom, had no windows and only one small door. The hut had a fire burning from the first of January until the thirty-first of December, as Grandma was always cold. When

I became of age, I had to fetch wood every day for the fire, and I also had to farm to provide food for Grandma and me. As a result, I had no childhood because my grandmother depended on me for a living.

There were times in my childhood when I had to beg for the bones that were meant for dogs in order to flavor our food with even the faintest taste of meat. Sometimes Grandma and I had no oil for cooking. I would work for my uncle, and he would give us a bottle of palm oil in return. Even when he refused to give us any oil, Grandma would still cook for him and give him food because he was her son.

I had to beg for school uniforms, books, and even a pen for writing. I had no sandals or shoes until I turned eleven years old. My first pair of shoes was the sandals of a missionary's seven-year-old daughter. My cousin was their cook, and they gave the sandals to him. He in turn gave them to me, but I was eleven years old and had to force my big feet into a seven-year-old's shoes.

One Saturday morning, I had to go to a farm that was about nine miles away. Grandma woke me up at 4:00 a.m. It was still dark, but I had to start early before the sun rose. It was also chilly, and since this took place before I had shoes, I walked barefoot along the dirt road. As I walked in the cold, tears streamed down my cheeks, but I had no choice except to obey. I gathered my courage and continued the dreadful journey.

About an hour into the trip, I suddenly heard someone demand, "Stop now and hand over your food and all you are carrying." An ex-army officer who was about six feet tall and very strong was speaking. He had been released from the military because of insanity. I was only a child, about four feet tall and weighing less than seventy pounds. Having suffered from kwashiorkor, I was malnourished and thus did not have the strength or ability to run away from him. I complied with his orders immediately.

The man then said, "I am going with you to the farm." I almost fainted from fright. All I could think about was that he might kill or rape me. I began to pray silently, *Oh God, deliver me like you delivered Daniel from the lions' den.* The Lord put the idea into my head to tell this man that I did not know where the farm was, but was going to meet an aunt who would take me there. Still undeterred, he insisted that he would go with me to my aunt's.

I turned into a nearby compound and knocked on the door. A woman answered, but when she saw the man standing there, she quickly shut the door. We kept going and approached another house. However, as soon as the people there saw us coming, they ran for their lives because the man with me was known to be extremely violent. We then encountered a woman cooking, and he asked if she was my aunt, to which I answered no.

"What are you going to do now?" he demanded.

With trembling lips, I answered, "I am no longer going to the farm."

"OK, take your stuff and return home immediately," he said.

"Yes, sir," I quickly replied and ran and hid in the bushes for a while. But then I thought to myself, "If I return home without going to the farm, we will starve. I have to go and harvest some sweet potatoes". So I eventually crawled out of the bushes and continued my journey. With God's help, I made it home safely.

Life grew increasingly difficult. I very much wanted to go to school, yet I had a grandmother to take care of. For me to obtain even the notebooks needed was difficult. I had to carry sand from a river to sell so as to get less than a dollar to buy my books. My father suggested to my stepbrother, who lived and worked in the city as an electrician, to take me in and send me to school. He agreed to the arrangement, but little did I know that I was jumping from the frying pan into the fire.

In the city, my suffering only multiplied. In order to earn money, I had to haul sugar cane after school every day, and I had to look for bottles, wash them, and sell them. To make matters worse, my stepbrother saw me as a slave for his own personal use. He was an alcoholic and would beat me until I passed out.

One day I refused to eat some stale food that my stepmother offered. Offended, she reported to her son that I had refused to eat because I had stolen a penny from the sugar-cane earnings, bought food, and eaten before I got home. The truth was that a group of people known as the "motor park boys" had taken some sugar cane from me without paying for it. When I got home, my stepmother counted the money, and it was short by a penny. For that I received a beating so severe that I passed out. I still bear the scar of that beating on my back to this very day.

When I finally regained consciousness, I was under my bed, and it was the next day. I crawled out, took a shower, and left for school. On my way, a driver who knew my mother saw me and asked if my mother had given me away as a sacrifice. When I arrived at school, I discovered, much to my dismay, there was no school that day. Youth Day had fallen on a Sunday, so today was a public holiday.

Feeling lonely and rejected, I thought of my life with my grandmother. She had nothing, yet there was so much love and laughter between us. In her home, I had a bamboo bed with nothing on it, yet I was happy and appreciated every good thing I did have. This thought so overwhelmed me that I could not help but cry.

As I sat by the road crying, an adult man passed by and asked me what was wrong. I told him the whole story. When he saw the blood and scars on my body, he advised me to run away and return to my grandmother. This would be a journey of twenty-five kilometers, which is about twenty miles. Nevertheless, I took to my heels and set off for my grandmother's house.

The trip was a whole day's journey. I had no water, no money, and no food. I was a young girl between eleven and twelve years old, and I began this journey like a runaway slave. Every time I heard people coming, I would jump into the bushes and hide until they passed. By the grace of Almighty God, I finally made it to my grandmother's house around eight o'clock that evening, feet swollen from the walking.

As soon as Grandma set eyes on me, she began to cry. We held each other for a long time, sobbing profusely. Then she looked down and saw my swollen feet, which looked like someone with elephantiasis. Immediately she warmed some water and began to bathe my feet with her tears and prayers.

Two days later, my stepmother came looking for me. I was so afraid that I climbed up into the roof of the house and hid. But my stepmother convinced my grandmother that they would never beat me again, and she pointed out that since it was the middle of the semester, I should return and finish out the term.

I desperately wanted an education so I could one day teach other poor children who were suffering. I also wanted to be able to work and take better care of my grandma, the elderly, and those who could not afford nutritious food or medication. I sincerely desired to be like Mother Teresa of Calcutta. To this very day, I still believe that God will one day bless me and allow me to be blessing to many less privileged children and people. I have to stop writing now because of the tears streaming down my face.

When I returned to Grandma, I was nothing more than a skeleton, but I was happy. Grandma prayed every morning from 5:00 a.m. to 6:00 a.m. On Sundays she took me to her Baptist church and made me sit by her until service was over. It lasted from 9:00 a.m. to 4:00 p.m. I got saved every Sunday at her church.

In all the challenges I faced growing up, the Lord made a way. When I was old enough, I took the entrance exam into college and passed. I wanted to go to a prestigious college called Our Lady of Lourdes, but I had only one dress. Early one morning, I washed it and put it back on. My aunt noticed the water dripping from it, and fearing I would catch pneumonia if I went out in a cold, wet dress, she called her daughter-in-law and asked her to lend me one of her dresses. She obliged, but the dress was a large XX in size, while I was a diminutive size 2.

When the white missionary at the school, the reverend sister, saw me in the oversized dress, she knew I was from a very poor family. She asked me about them and also asked what I would like to become in the future. I told her that my father was a king and had many wives and children. I shared that I wanted to get an education so I could help other children and also influence the government to pass a law that prohibited polygamy. A man should have only one wife, I felt, and they should have only the number of children that they could take care of.

The reverend sister saw the passion of my heart's cry and simply asked me if my father could afford my school fees. With excitement, I answered with a resounding yes. I believed that my father would do everything possible for me to attend this prestigious college. The reverend sister quickly signed a copy of the prospectus and gave it to me with a smile, saying, "See you when school resumes."

"Thank you very much," I responded. Then I knelt down, and she blessed me with the sign of the cross.

I ran out of the room in jubilant celebration. I could not wait for the bus to take me back to the village so I could present my admission letter and prospectus to my father. Everybody on the bus soon knew that I had been admitted, and they celebrated with me in song on our way home to the village. I was so happy that I did not care about the dust or the bumpy road. The joy of going to college was so much that I was not even hungry.

Arriving home, I handed the papers to my father, who was sick by this time. He asked me to read aloud the requirements for admission and the amount of money needed for tuition. As soon as I did, his countenance dropped, and he took the papers from my hands. We had a deadline to put down a deposit of ten thousand CFA francs, or approximately a thousand dollars.

As the deadline approached, I went to my father to remind him. To my great dismay, he had been tearing the papers and using them to wrap his tobacco for cigarettes. I left his presence crying and asking God why. I wanted to commit suicide, and I stopped going to school. I became so depressed and rebellious that I actually failed my first School Leaving Certificate

Exam. I told myself despairingly, *"Why should I work hard to pass when I am not going to college anyway?"*

Chapter 2

Life with My Elder Sister Ma Alice

At this point in my life, my older sister, who shared the same mother as I, arrived in the village. Like me, she had finished primary school, but there was nobody to send her to college. Consequently, she had been sent to the village to get married. The little money that my father did have was used to educate the boys, not the girls. Please bear in mind that in those days, the female children of a family were regarded primarily as commodities.

Thanks be to God for my sister, who refused to get married at the age of sixteen or seventeen. Instead, she earned money by carrying sand and selling it, and eventually she returned to town. There she got a job with a company called the Cameroon Development Corporation and began to work as a nursing assistant. She now requested that I come and stay with her and go back to school. God bless her for that. But she had to remain firm in order to get me away from my father, who was expecting me to get married also at an early age. But my sister persisted, and I moved in with her.

Grandmothers have a way of pampering their grand-children so that they leave an indelible mark. So had my grandmother done with me. Life was better with my sister, but her commanding voice, coupled with a no-pampering attitude, often left me in tears and longing for my grandmother.

However, two specific incidents with my sister changed my character for life. During the first inci-dent, I had taken an old towel to the black bush, a very dense rainforest, in order to carry some plantains home. I gathered the fruit and began the walk home, struggling under the heavy load that I was carrying. As I attempted to adjust the cushioning on my head, the towel fell. When my sister returned home and discovered what had happened, she shouted and rebuked me.

I became angry with my sister and refused to eat, thinking that she would soon beg me to eat as Grandma had always done. Instead, the opposite occurred: she locked her kitchen so I could not have access to any food. When I packed up my things to return to Grandma, she beat me. To this very day, no matter how angry I am, I never refuse food from my elders.

The second incident occurred when a family that was even poorer than we were needed some oil for cooking. The man's wife had a baby, yet they were trying to cook their food without oil. When she begged me for oil, I gave her the whole container. When my sister discovered that I had given the oil away, she gave me another beating.

I finally repeated the school year and passed. Since my sister did not make enough money to send me to a private college, such as Saker or Our Lady of Lourdes, I had to study and pass the Government Entrance Exam in List A. Those on list A who passed the exam went on to government colleges, where they got some type of scholarship or basically a free education. All that their sponsors had to do was buy the school supplies and pay a minimal fee.

I attended many interviews and was eventually accepted, but our poverty caused my sister to prefer a technical college for me. For the first year, I had to walk six miles daily to and from school. I lived with extended family members who could barely feed themselves. Thus, I resorted once more to farming and begging for bones meant for dogs to have a meal with a little flavor of meat in it.

At one time, I went to live with another stepmother during Christmas vacation so that I could help her in the cocoa harvest. The agreement was that at the end of the holidays, she would assist me with my school needs. I arrived at her house around ten in the evening, having stayed fourteen hours at the motor park, where the cost for a car had doubled since it was peak season. I had 250 CFA francs in my possession, but the fare to my stepmother's would cost 500 CFA francs.

The driver who finally brought me to my stepmother's did so out of compassion. He had made several trips that day and had noticed me sitting with no food to eat and no water to drink. Had I used any of my money to buy food, I would have had even less for my fare. On his last trip to the village, he agreed to take me for only 250 CFA francs. I was so grateful to him for his kindness and to God for His provision.

When this man drove by the next morning, I recognized his car and shouted another thank you to him. Hearing my voice, he stopped, but he did not recognize me and asked, "Who are you?" I told him that I was the girl he had carried for half the fare the day before. He exclaimed that he did not recognize me because mosquito bites had so marred my face. He was so compassionate that he bought a mosquito repellant called Moon Tiger for me and instructed me to burn it near my bed at bedtime.

Bear in mind that the house where I was staying was constructed of tree bark, and the roof was made of palm fronds. Furthermore, the bed had a grass mattress. Burning a mosquito coil in that environment would have been a risky move. As a result, mosquitoes fed on me for the one month I stayed there. The good news is that I was able to sell some farm products during that time, as I pushed a hand truck full of cassava, sweet potatoes, and vegetables to market.

The road to the market square is a story of its own. In one instance, I arrived at the foot of a hill and wasn't strong enough to push the cart upward, so I decided to pull it instead. In so doing, I slipped and fell. The fall was so bad that I had to let go of the cart, and it rolled all the way down the hill and overturned. I sprained my leg in the fall and had to limp down the hill in pain and tears to gather my produce. If I did not sell the vegetables, I would not have money to go back to school. I needed that money for lotion, soap, a pack of sugar for my garri, and transportation. But God is always faithful, and He saw me through.

Back in school, because I did very well, I was granted admission into the dormitory. In addition to my school uniform, I had only one dress to wear. This dress had been given to me by my elder sister, who wore size X, while I was a size 0. I looked like a skeleton in that dress, and students made fun of me every time I wore it. Consequently, I could not attend parties or participate in other functions; all I did, other than attend class, was to go to church.

My worst days in school were visiting Sundays. These were the days set aside for family and friends to spend the afternoon with their loved ones at the school. Families would bring food, soda, and goodies and eat with the ones that had come to see. But no one came to visit me, so I would carry my books and go sit under a mango tree. There I would look up to heaven with tears in my eyes and pray to God: "Please, Papa God, help me." I would pray that one day I would be able to help children who had nobody or had parents too poor to provide them with the necessities of life.

Needless to say, the birds and butterflies became my friends. I found in nature my entertainment. I talked to the ants, butterflies, birds, and, above all, God, whom I could not see. But my grandmother had taught me that He was ever present with me. I can assure you that He is a silent yet attentive listener. I always verbalized my feelings to Him, that one day I would be very rich and help as many people as He would enable me to assist. God, my creator and the great waymaker, did make a way for me, and I finally graduated from the school.

Chapter 3

Married out of Necessity

I got married, not out of love, but out of necessity. I wanted to continue my education and found a man who offered to help. After this man saw my school performance, he promised to assist me further in my education if I married him. Desperate for his help, I accepted his offer, ignoring our age difference. He did keep his promise, but after we were married, I discovered that he had six children with four other women, instead of the three children that he had told me about.

Being born into a polygamous family, I loved children. I still believe that there can be a wrong sexual relationship, but never a wrong child. Every child is a gift from God and must be given a chance to manifest his or her destiny. King Solomon was born as a result of an unacceptable marriage, yet God blessed him with unusual wisdom. So I accepted this man's children and began to take care of them.

But I had no child of my own. One day after the death of my mother-in-law, I heard people gossiping about my childlessness, and their cruel words made me cry. The insult was especially hard to bear coming from a young girl that I was sponsoring in college. As a result, I was determined to find a solution to end my barrenness. I chased after anyone and everyone who promised a solution. It did not matter where I had to go and what the cost would be. I went everywhere for medical advice, even to a witch doctor. But everyone gave me a negative report, and most of them, preying upon my desperation, exploited me financially, materially, and emotionally. Please remember to be careful when you are desperate.

One of the instances when I was taken advantage of occurred on a bright Saturday morning. Shortly after my husband and I arrived at the airport, a cab driver picked us up and took us straight to a native doctor. Little did we know that the driver, whom we thought was an angel taking us to our destination, was actually an agent of darkness.

I wasn't the only person visiting the witch doctor that day, but I was the last client on this particular day. When I entered the room, a spirit with the voice of an old woman spoke through a human skull and greeted me audibly. This was the first time I had ever experienced something like that, and I quickly realized that not all the beings we meet are human beings. The spirit said that the doctor would not have time to see me because it was market day and she was leaving to do her shopping.

The skull also demanded to know why I was angry. Indeed, I was very angry, because while sitting there, I thought to myself, "Is my case so bad that the spirit of a dead person has to speak to me?" The skull then said it was going to my father's house to investigate the cause of my barrenness. In less than a minute, it came back with an answer.

In order to convince me to believe in the diagnosis, the spirit began to describe my mother's kitchen: where the water pot was placed and where the cooking area was located. Needless to say, I was shocked at the accuracy of the description. My eyes opened wide, and my anger turned to amazement. I sat up straight and paid close attention.

According to the spirit's findings, I was to have been a twin. I had a twin brother who was not born; he was in the sea and was very jealous of me. The spirit behind the skull said that my twin brother was the cause of my barrenness, and the only way to appease him was to offer an animal sacrifice. The spirit proceeded to say that he (my brother) was requesting a dog to be slaughtered over my head at midnight in a river close by a sea.

Hearing those words, my heart seemed to stop for a moment, and I felt like I would faint. I am a passionate animal lover, and to think that I would have to sacrifice a dog just so I could have a child was nearly more than I could bear. When I was growing up, my father had two dogs that were treated like his own children; and to top it all off, a dog had saved me from a venomous snake when I was a child.

On that occasion, my mother had taken me to the farm and set me under a tree to sleep while she worked. As I lay there, the snake slowly crept towards me. However, our dog ran to my mother and alerted her to the danger. When she saw the snake, she ran to get my father. The dog stood there barking furiously at the snake while she was gone, which distracted it from biting me until my father arrived and killed it. But for this dog, I would have died.

How, then, was I now going to kill a dog in order to appease a twin brother that I had never seen and would never see? He was unknown to me, and none of it made any sense. However, God is faithful; He later gave me a second chance to follow Him wholeheartedly and opened my eyes to the truth forever.

Wedding Pictures

Miracle Ruth Edison

Chapter 4

In Search of a Child

The expression of horror was so visible on my face that the witch doctor and cab driver intervened and said, "If you do this, nine months from today you will be breast-feeding your own child." That assurance calmed me. But then came the fee: the spirit named the exact amount of money we had saved to print my husband's book. In fact, he was soon to go to Lagos to print the book, which had taken us years to save up for. My husband, his hands shaking, opened his brief-case and handed the witch doctor all the money. At this point, I could no longer hold back my tears. Even now as I write, tears of regret still flow from my eyes.

The witch doctor then instructed us to go buy a dog and bring it back. Obtaining a dog was another challenge, so the cab driver, who was a native of the area, took us on a dog hunt. What I saw with my eyes, my mouth cannot express in words. The experience was so terrifying that we almost gave up, but we could not, for the sake of our nonrefundable savings that we had already given up. About 6:00 p.m., we finally secured a dog, which we then took back to the witch doctor.

Around 11:00 p.m., we left for the hour's drive to the river. Exactly at midnight, I undressed and stood in the river while four men lifted the dog over my head and slaughtered it. As soon as the warm blood of the innocent animal touched my head, I fainted on the inside. In my heart, I felt like I had killed a human being. After the ceremony was completed, I was given concoctions to bathe with every morning, something to put under my bed, and some leaves to put into wine and drink three times a day: once in the morning, once in the afternoon, and once in the evening. Thus in the process of trying to have a baby, I became an alcoholic.

God have mercy, but lack of knowledge is man's worst enemy. Please, as you read this book, commit to fight ignorance with all your might. God said His people perish from lack of knowledge. You are suffering from what you do not know, so pant after knowledge like a deer panting after water. Knowledge will deliver you from unnecessary trauma, death, and endless pain.

Two weeks after the dreadful treatment, the expected pregnancy did not take place. In fact, my menstrual cycle came two weeks earlier than usual. I was devastated; after all I had gone through, I still had no baby to show for it. That was when I became an emotional wreck. Nobody could feel or share my pain. Many nights I sobbed quietly while my husband slept and snored next to me. Other nights I had to go to the restroom and shut the door so that I could cry out loud. Sometimes I cried so loudly that I was grateful for the soundproof walls in our house.

After two months of faithfully but fruitlessly performing the rituals, I decided to put an end to it all. At this point, I was ready to commit suicide; the pressure was just too much to bear. The insults from my sisters-in-law had become intolerable. They called me "another man" and "a dry tree." They demanded that their brother marry another woman, and according to the culture, I would have to pay her bride price.

The thought of my husband taking another wife did not register well with me, mostly because of what I had watched my mother go through. My father was a king who married many wives who bore him many children that he could not properly care for. One of my greatest fights remains against polygamy. I do not support the idea of a man marrying more than one wife. My prayer is that God will bless me and give me wealth to go into the world and fight this cultural tradition. I want to educate young girls and equip them to make a living without depending on a man for everything or feeling forced by poverty to become some man's fifth or seventh wife.

To end it all, I gathered all the tablets of medication in the house. I did not care what they were for or why they were there. I collected quite a few and knew if I took all of them, it would all be over. While I was still contemplating how to take the pills, a thought came to me: "Go see your gynecologist before you do it so that that your family will not blame your husband for killing you."

Heeding the thought, I went to see my gynecologist, and he said, "Let's do one more scan before I talk to you." After the scan, he sat me down, took a puff on his cigarette, and said, "Madame, your situation is very bad. I cannot help you, and there is no one I know who can help you except God. We doctors do not give children—only God does." With that he took another puff on the cigarette and blew the smoke towards the heavens as if to say, "Pray to the God of heaven to help you."

Right there in his office, I fainted. When I finally recovered, my husband was called to take me home and make me rest. However, as soon as we got home, I began to cry again. My husband became so infuriated that he challenged me. "You have many Bibles, and you pray a lot. Can't you just pray one prayer and ask your God to solve your problem? I am sick and tired of your crying." After this statement, he slammed the door and left to go out to a club to enjoy himself.

I was crying hysterically and looking for the tablets to commit suicide when my doorbell rang. I quickly wiped my tears and ran to the door. It was my favorite stepsister, Mary. The moment I opened the door, she slumped into my arms and burst into tears. I thought somebody had died, so I joined her in her grief, and we cried together for a good thirty minutes. Then I asked her, "Who died?" and she responded, "Nobody."

By now I was both confused and curious, so I asked Mary, "Then why are you crying?" and she replied, "I am crying because a man deceived me and told me that he would marry me and take me to America. I gave in to him, and now I am pregnant with another child and he is nowhere to be found. I am going to have an abortion, and if I die in the process, take care of my first son."

"Oh no, sister!" I shouted. "You cannot do that. I want a child, so please keep this pregnancy and deliver the baby and give it to me. I will take the baby and raise it as my own." Before she finally settled down, I had promised to pay all the bills and buy everything necessary in preparation for the birth. Then she ate some food and spent some time with me before heading back home.

Chapter 5

The Turning Point

I went to my room, fell on my knees, and prayed fervently. "Father God," I said, "I thank You that I have a baby coming through my sister. Dear God, I pray You will give me love for this child as though I were the biological mother, but God, if You know that someday in the future someone will insult me for being a barren woman, then give me my own. But if You created me to be childless, help me not to be jealous of others. Thank You Father God, for I pray in Jesus Christ's name. Amen."

As soon as I ended my prayer, I heard a voice say to me, "Clean your house." I replied, "The house was vacuumed this morning." Then the voice said, "No, I mean throw away all the things the witch doctor gave you, and forgive everyone who has offended you. Then fast for three days and pray Isaiah 54:1–17."

Mind you, I had never fasted a day in my life. I liked food. Three meals a day was my lifestyle; after all, I had a very good cook. However, I immediately obeyed and threw away everything the witch doctor had given me and began to release and forgive all my enemies. I started the fast the very next day. I took in no water and no food, and I separated myself from my husband.

Everything was going well until the last night leading into the third day. Then, for the first time during my fast, my husband raised hell. He said if I did not yield to his demands, I should pack my things and go. The marriage was over, he said. Nevertheless, I stood my ground, thinking, For seven good years, I have never said no to you. So why all this fire and brimstone just for two nights?

I quickly ran to the guest room, and of course he followed me and tore off my nightgown. I then ran naked to the living room, shouting for help, and he retreated. I then spent the rest of the night alone in the guest room.

In the daytime, it was the cook's turn. He had noticed that for almost three days I had not eaten anything. He took it upon himself to prepare my favorite food, a Cameroonian delicacy that takes a long time to prepare because of the intricate process involved. The cook prepared the dish of shrimp, smoked fish, and smoked meat, and the irresistible aroma wafted through the house. I had to leave the house to keep from giving in and took a mat with me to sit under a mango tree so as to avoid the temptation.

While I was sitting under the tree, the cook dished up the food and brought it to me. As soon as I glanced at the food, my mouth watered. There and then, I heard in my spirit, "Man does not live by bread alone." A new strength came into me, and I said, "No, thank you. Take it back. I cannot eat now." The cook began to cry, assuming he had done something wrong and I was going to fire him. I tried to explain as best I could. "I am not mad at you," I assured him. "Just go for now, and I will tell you later my reason for not eating." He refused to give up the issue and leave me alone, so I walked away.

The fight with my husband and my cook show that nothing of great value comes easily. By the grace of God, 6:00 p.m. finally came, and I knelt beside my bed and prayed. "Father God," I said, "I know that I have not been perfect in this fast, but to the best of my ability, I have tried. Forgive and have mercy on me where I have failed. In Jesus Christ's name, I pray. Amen."

Then I heard a gentle voice say, "Ask for the sex of the child you would like to have first." I said I wanted a girl. I wanted a girl because my mother in-law, who had been so good to me, had died, and I wanted to name the child after her. Then I heard, "Peace be with you."

Immediately a heavy weight lifted from me, and the peace that surpasses all understanding permeated my body. I felt so light and free that I thought I could fly. I could not contain my joy and wanted to tell my sister about it. When I walked out of the room and toward her, she was about five feet away. Startled, she quickly stepped backward and asked, "Who is that man standing behind you?" Then she asked me another question: "What is that light shining over you?" More questions followed, and she kept stepping backward as she tried to make sense of what was happening.

Confused by my sister's questions, I looked behind me to see who was there, but I saw no one.

Whatever it was that had taken place was so tangible that when I got to college the next day, all my students noticed my glowing countenance. I could see the amazement on their faces. Some of the other teachers also noticed and asked me what had happened. "It seems like somebody peeled off your skin and now your complexion is lighter," they said. "Tell us the name of the secret cream that has transformed and rejuvenated you like this."

I just smiled and said, "It is just the peace of the Lord Jesus Christ." I could not explain any more than that because I could not even comprehend it myself. All day long, it was as if I were walking on air.

Chapter 6

The Miracle

A month went by—no menses; two weeks more, and still no menses. My husband noticed that my package of feminine pads remained unopened, and I had not complained of any cramping, as I usually did. He asked, "Have you noticed that it's been six weeks since you've had your period?" He looked at the chart and pointed it out to me and then added, "Please go see your doctor tomorrow."

I first said no to his request, fearful that the doctor might say I was in early menopause. When a week went by and I still had not had my period, my husband became even more concerned. He begged me to do a pregnancy test, but I refused. Early one morning when

I went to use the restroom, he entered with a bottle and instructed, "Put some of your urine in here for me." I laughed so hard at his request, but I did as he asked. He then took the sample to a friend who was a lab technician. At the lab, his friend ran three different types of pregnancy tests on it.

A short time later, we were at the table eating breakfast when the doorbell began to ring continuously, as if someone had something urgent to be brought to our attention. My husband opened the door, and while still standing outside, the lab technician shouted, "She is pregnant! Pregnant! Pregnant! You did it! You did it!"

My husband lifted his friend from the ground as if he were the one who had put the baby in my womb. He ushered the man inside our home and quickly surrendered his breakfast plate to him. He said, "My brother, take all you want on this table. In fact, take my seat. I am so happy with this good news that I am not hungry anymore."

He then turned to me and smiled, saying, "Please hurry and get dressed. Let's go see your doctor for a scan." Confused and feeling as if I were dreaming, I left the food on my plate, quickly got dressed, and immediately headed for the doctor's office.

When the doctor saw us, he was alarmed and asked my husband, "What's happening? Is your wife in pain?"

My husband quickly replied, "No, doctor, I just want you to scan her because it has been almost two months since she had a period."

The doctor replied, "Oh no, it may be early menopause! Well, it's your money. Come on in and pay, and then I'll do the scan."

We did as he instructed, and shortly after he turned on the machine, he exclaimed, "I cannot believe it! It is a miracle—come and see. It's true—she is pregnant. That's the fetus; listen to its heartbeat. This is unbelievable! It can only be a miracle. I will never again tell a woman that she cannot ever have a child, for God still does miracles. I now believe that with God all things are possible. Congratulations, sir. Your wife is indeed pregnant. At last your wait is over."

It was then that I knew this was not a dream. It was for real. Praise be to God! All through the pregnancy I stayed very healthy. I still did all the things I always did up to my seventh month.

One day my husband scheduled a trip, so I dropped him off at the airport. When I got home, I met up with my sister-in-law, the one who had earlier insulted me. As soon as she saw me so obviously pregnant, she almost fainted from surprise. She immediately picked up her bags and left. She told everyone living in our house in the village, and one of them packed and relocated to another village.

My sister Mary, who was also pregnant, continued to encourage me. Like Elizabeth and Mary in the Bible, we were expecting at the same time. My sister delivered a month before me and named her baby Bridget, after me. My turn came on January 24, 1991, when my daughter was born in Mount Mary hospital in Buea, Cameroon.

The news quickly spread all over town, and even a madman came to see the long-awaited miracle. This man gave me five hundred CFA francs to buy clothes for the baby. So many people were flocking in to see my child that the hospital staff had to control the traffic into my room. At one time, the doctor encountered as many as twenty people in my room.

Jehovah is a miracle-working God. Aware of that fact, I named my child Miracle Ruth Edison. I chose Miracle for obvious reasons: born against all odds, she was indeed a miracle wrought by the mighty act of God. I selected Ruth for her middle name because I wanted my Jehovah God to also be her God. Her birth proved that God indeed answers sincere and fervent prayers.

My daughter's arrival brought great joy into my life and strengthened my faith in the Lord. When she turned three, however, my marriage began to experience some storms. I vividly recall one day during that turbulent time when my miracle baby prayed for me. Coming into my room, she found me on my knees, crying to God for an urgent answer. "Mommy, why are you crying?" my little girl asked.

"Baby, I have too many bills to pay, and your father has refused to help me," I tried to explain.

My husband had been transferred to his hometown, and he visited Miracle and me only every once in a while. But I needed money for rent and food and had many mouths to feed. I had started a prayer cell in my house, which soon became a center of refuge. Many people came for prayer, and some of them stayed.

Some of them came from afar, with nothing to their names and no money to get back home. I had to feed them while they were with me, and then I had to pay their transportation fees back home. Their needs were genuine, and I wanted to help; but my income was insufficient for all the many needs.

When Miracle saw me crying that day, she laid her little hand on me and said, "Don't cry! You told me we have a miracle-working God. He will give you a miracle." Then she prayed, as if in tongues, and finished with "In Jesus name, Amen." She then gave me a hug and left the room.

In less than an hour, my doorbell rang. A Reverend Father from my village stood on the doorstep. He was the instrument God used to answer my little girl's prayer. He brought bags of rice, beans, meat, chicken, trays of eggs, and two gallons of oil, and he also gave me enough money to pay all my bills, with excess remaining. God still answers prayer, especially the prayers of children. That is why Jesus told His disciples, "Allow the children to come to me, for such is the Kingdom of God." I urge you today to hand over all your problems to God in prayer. Just trust Him, and He will come through for you.

Chapter 7

Unbearable Storms

The storms in my marriage kept growing. My husband did not like the fact that I no longer cuddled with him at night. Furthermore, I no longer consulted mediums or consumed alcohol like I used to do. I was truly a changed woman. Thus, the persecution from him began.

Our approach to issues was very different, so when he decided to take Miracle with him to his new station, I quit my job and joined him. When I got there, the persecution only intensified. He had rebuilt his Amoc altar in our bedroom. He forbade me to pray or fast, and he asked me to stop going to church. He demanded that I denounce my beliefs and become a member of his cult, but my reply was firm and resolute: "When I needed a child, I did all that, and it did not help me. I cannot go back, because I have discovered a better way. This way is Jesus Christ, our Lord and Savior" (see John 3:16).

The tension between us intensified. It got to the point that when I lay in bed next to him, he would become restless, complaining many times that fire from my body was burning him. I should stop praying, even in my heart, he said. Amazingly, despite his accusation, I was not even praying, but the greater One living inside me, the Holy Spirit of God, would not allow him to be at peace.

My husband would often wake up in the middle of the night and do invocations and incantations for demonic spirits to attack me. But the power of God and His presence in my life were so prevalent that the demons would not come. My husband's uneasiness got so bad that he eventually banished me from the room, and I took to sleeping on a chair facing the room. Still tormented, he removed the chair, so then I slept on the floor facing our room. This went on for many months until he could not take it anymore.

My husband wrote a letter and asked me to choose between Jesus and him. If I chose my Lord Jesus over him, the marriage would be over, and I would not be allowed to take three-year-old Miracle with me. That day of decision was the longest day of my entire life. I was caught between pleasing God and preserving my marriage.

I thought of many things that day. For example, how could I preach about the fruits of the Spirit, one of which is longsuffering, if I was not willing to be tested in those areas? I also knew from reading my Bible that God hates divorce (Malachi 3:16). Even though my husband and I had married before I became a Christian, I was determined to make my marriage work. Also, I had married him against the wishes of my mother and family and did not want to prove them right. Furthermore, he had come into my life after my own father had died and filled a father role for me. Finally, he had not only encouraged but also assisted me in my last year of school.

My grandmother, who was a Baptist Christian, had always told me to do for others what you want them to do for you. I was in a dilemma. What would people say if my marriage failed? I had preached and counseled others when they faced marital challenges, so if my marriage didn't make it, people were sure to ask, "How come you could not practice what you preached in your own marriage?"

Caught in this web, I made the only choice I could. I decided to live my life to please God to the best of my knowledge and ability. I prayed like never before, but the more I prayed and gave it my best, the worse my marriage became. The persecution grew so unbearable that my husband and I could not see eye to eye on anything. It came to the point that he would not even look at my face when we sat at the table to eat. Fire, he said, was coming out of my eyes and hitting his forehead. We were like a cat and dog with each other.

Please, do not judge those who have divorced. Only God knows who married for the right or wrong reasons. I want to advise you, though, that if you are married and going through storms, hold on because storms do not last forever. Do all within your power to make your marriage work, especially if there are children are involved.

Whenever two elephants fight, the grass around them is trampled. Children of divorced parents always suffer something. Nonetheless, if you have done your best and know before God that your conscience is clear, you must let the marriage go if your life is at risk. One thing you must know in advance, though, is that people will always have something to say about you. Just make sure on your part that you have done everything you could to the best of your ability.

The straw that broke the camel's back for me came one day when I took Miracle to Christ Apostolic Church, which had been founded by my late mother-in-law, a committed Christian. I found comfort and peace every time I went to the church and fellowshiped with the brethren there. When I got back home that day, my husband ordered me to leave his house and return to my parents, but he said I could not take his daughter. Furthermore, I was not to take any extra clothes, only what I had on. In Africa, divorce does not favor the woman. She is considered merely the property of her husband.

When my husband issued this ultimatum, I ran to him and fell on my knees, crying and begging him to give me another chance. "I promise to do better," I pleaded. I even called for our little daughter to beg her dad for me, but of course she was too young to understand what was going on. Doll in hand, she drew closer, standing and looking at her parents, wiping the tears from her mother's eyes.

I had nowhere to go and no one to talk to but God, so I went on a three-day fast. I went to the church for each of the three days, calling on the Lord God to intervene and change my husband's heart. "But Lord," I said, "if he refuses, then I will not leave without my daughter." After all, he had six other children besides Miracle.

The God of miracles came through again around 4:00 p.m. on that fateful Saturday. As I looked up from the floor mat where I was lying, I saw the word *TIME* written in gold capital letters. I can still see it now as I am writing this book. I tried to pronounce it like a familiar name in my region that was spelled the same, but I heard a voice audibly say it for me: "Time." Knowing beyond a shadow of a doubt that God had answered my prayer, I was prompted to go home.

Upon my arrival, my husband greeted me with a smile and said, "I have changed my mind. You can take our daughter and some of her clothes with you. You take care of her and pay for her school until she is ready to go to college. Do not ask me for a penny."

I quickly replied, "Thank you, sir," and I made my plans to leave. Now all I needed was a boat to bring me to the mainland, where I could take a taxi to my family. Surprisingly, my husband volunteered to transport us to the town where we were headed. When we got to the motor park in that town, he kissed his daughter good-bye and put a thousand CFA francs into her hands.

I had no money of my own and nowhere to go. My daughter and I were homeless, so I took a taxi to my sister Mary, who worked as a nursing assistant in the projects. She had a one-bedroom place for her and her children and could barely provide for her own family. Now here I was, adding to her burden.

At Mary's home, restrooms where located outside and used by everybody. The environment was so filthy that Miracle refused to come out of the house for four whole days. She cried and begged, "Mommy, let's go home!"

In response to her pleading, I cried and tried to explain our new circumstances. "Baby, we have no home," I said, "but one day God will bless Mommy to own a house."

Then she tried another tactic. "Mommy, I need TV," she said, to which I replied, "Baby, just a little while and then Mommy will bounce back and life will be better than ever." I prayed and cried and prayed some more.

One day I borrowed some money and went to see a friend who had a business in Douala, Cameroon. By the grace of God, she hired me. On my way back home to make preparations for the job, I met my beloved sister in the Lord, Helen Fonachu. She was a woman with whom I had often prayed. We both suffered from marital difficulties, but we loved the Lord so much that we only served Him all the more. We were ready to go to any length for Christ.

Helen had taken in her brother, who was insane, and we had prayed to God until his sanity was restored. Whenever either of our husbands made a surprise visit home, Helen's brother, Moah, who was getting better, would report us to them. In his own words, he would say, "Sir, as soon as you leave this house now, church for my head." He was trying to say, "As soon as you leave this house, they are going to lay hands on my head and start praying for me."

A funny thing happened one day when Helen's dog followed a female evangelist to a neighbor's house, where we had obtained a bedroom for her use. The dog killed the widower's hen and chicks, so the man decided to bring the dead chicken to Dr. Fonachu and my husband and expose the truth of what he thought was going on. "Sir," he said to the two men, "your wives have started a church in this house. They are pretending to be Presbyterians, but they are born again. During the week when you are not here, this whole place is filled with people from all walks of life and from all over. They have church every day."

"Moreover, they have even hired a pastor from Nigeria, for whom they have rented a room in my house. That is the reason your dog came and killed my chicken. Pay me, because I was growing the chicken to pay my children's school fees." He got his wish and was was paid ten thousand CFA francs. As soon as our husbands left to go to the club, Helen and I had to load up the evangelist's possessions and move her to another place.

Despite all our trials, we were unstoppable. The more we were persecuted, the stronger and more determined we became. We set our faces like flint, and our minds were made up. We were going all the way with God. For us it was either Jesus or nothing at all; and His grace was powerful and sufficient for us, never once failing.

That same week, as if what had happened with the evangelist was not enough, we ministered to a pregnant sister in Christ who was being oppressed by demonic spirits. She was taken to the hospital to be operated upon because the pregnancy had lasted more than seventeen months. As soon as the news of this dear sister reached us, we left our own babies in the care of others and set out for the remote village where the woman lived.

The road to the village was plowed by a truck once a day, and it was not in good shape. On some parts of the road, we had to stop and push the truck out of the mud. But thanks be to God, we finally arrived in the village at 3:00 a.m. We prayed with the woman and set off for home, getting there around 7:00 a.m. We went on to work that day as if we had just gotten up from a good night's sleep in our own beds. To this day, my friend and I refer to this adventure as the "Entebbe raid."

No matter what Justice Helen and I went through, we maintained our love for the Lord. This made us closer than sisters from the womb. Miracle even called her "Mother" because all through secondary school and high school, she lived with Justice Helen, who regarded our household and family as her immediate family.

Now, let me get back to where I was going to get my things to start my new job. Anyway, at the taxi park, the fight to secure a taxi was so intense that I was pushed out of the vehicle I was boarding and fell. As I stood by the roadside weeping, Helen was passing by in her car and recognized me. She quickly stopped and offered me a ride. I then told her what had befallen me, how I had been given an ultimatum to choose between the Lord Jesus Christ and my husband and had chosen the Lord, thus ending my marriage. I cried as I related the sad story, and she joined in and cried with me.

At the end, however, she said, "Weep no more. Like He did with Joseph, God is taking you somewhere great. This is just a training session. When God has finished training you, your name will become a household word. Many will read your story and marvel at the wonder-working power of your God. They will worship the Lord Jesus Christ because of you. Please don't give up, but be strong and courageous. God is with you; just hold on to Him. He will never let you down." She then burst into tongues and prayed for me with all her might. As we parted in tears, I was more determined than ever to serve God.

With all my strength, I started my new job, but I still had evening prayers after work. Mrs. Rita F. gave me a room on the second floor of the shop, which was soon transformed into a prayer and deliverance room. People came from all over to receive prayer. It was here that I met Pastor Ignatius, who took me under his wing and made his pulpit available to me. During worship he would play his guitar while the rest of us joyfully clapped our hands. We did not have a fancy church, but we had the power of God. We saw signs, wonders, and deliverances beyond description. In great and mighty ways, God confirmed His word.

It was in this city that one day, a sister asked me to drop her off at the airport. She was traveling to Nigeria for the Women's Anglo Conference. On the way, I was talking to her about some great men of God from Nigeria: Archbishop Benson Idahosa, Dr. Oduyemi, Dr. Kumuyi, and Bishop Oyedepo. When we arrived at the ticketing area, my friend introduced me to Reverend Dr. (Mrs.) Rosaline Oduyemi, and she immediately invited me to Bethel Wonder City Church. When I went, Sister Helen provided the ticket. The trip was supposed to last a weekend, but it ended up lasting three months.

God did wonders during my time at Bethel. Papa Gabriel was the first pastor to give me a tithe of tithes. He even offered me a good-paying job at the church. I knew I needed to seek God about this potentially life-changing decision, so I locked myself in the house for seven days while I prayed and fasted. I wanted the mind of God.

On the seventh day, I had an out-of-body encounter. It went on for a while, and I completely lost track of time. In the vision, a man of God named Papa Adeboye was praying and laying hands on a very long line of people. When he got to me, he told me to wait and he would come back to me. Finally, when he laid hands on me, he said the following words: "You shall go to nations. Be not afraid, for the Lord will go before you and do signs and wonders through you." I was frightened by this experience because I had never entered into this spiritual dimension before, but I knew the Lord was calling me to the nations of the world. I then decided to return to Cameroon. Dr. Oduyemi had given me 150,000 CFA francs prior to my trip to Nigeria. I had attended a program at the Full Gospel Church. The guest speaker, Dr. Dawne Collins, was a missionary from America. He spoke stirringly about how Christians must be the true light of the world by being productive and helping their communities. He so challenged me to do more for my community and for mankind as a whole.

When the service ended, I thanked him for inspiring me to think outside the box and for challenging me to serve God more by serving other people and the community. I told him that I wanted to do just that but needed more education in order to be effective. He shared with me that he was the president of American Indian University, and I responded that I would like to go to his school but could not afford it at the time. I asked him to give me two years, and I would work very hard and save enough money to go to his school. He then took my address.

As soon as I could, I sent the first fifteen hundred dollars through my beloved spiritual sister Rita. She and her husband then added another fifteen hundred dollars, so now I had three thousand dollars sent to AIC for my registration. As soon as I returned from Nigeria, I was told that a letter from America had arrived for me. It was a Form I-20 for requesting a student visa. In hopes of securing the necessary visa, I then traveled to Yaoundé, the capital of Cameroon, where the Embassy of the United States of America is located.

In Yaoundé the brother of my friend challenged my God. He said that if I was granted a visa, he would believe in my God. As if this were not enough, a German woman who had come to Cameroon for a visit also said, "If they give you a visa to go to the United States, I will follow you to church." With that in mind, I got up at midnight and prayed, "Oh Lord, for the sake of these two souls, let them give me the visa."

How I thank God for the blessed late Sister Helen. She went with me to the embassy the next day. While we were waiting in line, I began to pray for a girl who was dumb and deaf. I said, "Lord, if there is one visa to be given today, then let it be for this deaf and dumb girl." I soon heard my name called and walked up to the window.

The Lord had gone before me. My sister in Christ, Mrs. Rita, had faxed a bank statement to the embassy. I had no large file of documentation with me, only the letter about the student visa and a few papers. But God touched the hearts of those at the embassy, and I was granted a visa. I was then told that I would have to pay ten thousand CFA francs for the visa, but I had only five thousand. I walked over to a bank and said, "Sir, I have just been given a visa, but I have only five thousand CFA francs. Please, could you give me five thousand more?" He called his wife to discuss it, and they agreed to give me the money needed. I got the visa and left for America within two weeks, already two weeks late for school. Praise God for my friends and sisters in Christ who stood with me!

After receiving the visa, I ran to the home of a family friend and called my sister to let her know that I would stop by for a day or two to see our mother. My mother had not believed that I would be granted a visa. She had always wanted me to become a medical doctor and denounce my preaching, and the quarrel between us because of my choice of career had strained our relationship. In fact, it was so bad that she had refused to touch my child, because she did not want anything to do with this radical woman who had left every comfort to follow Jesus Christ. She had once said that if I stopped what I was doing, she would send me to America, but of course I refused. I said that when I wanted to go to America, my God would make a way. When she heard that I had obtained a visa, she called three other relatives to verify it. God indeed had done it without her help. God is great. With Him all things are possible.

On August 26, I went to the airport with an entourage of about twenty-five people. My precious Miracle and Bridget, who were then only four, were not there. Because of my ignorance of the real America, I promised all my relatives and well-wishers who came to the airport to see me off that every month I would send them money. I thought dollars were just waiting to be picked up on the streets of America. I told them to wipe away their tears because poverty in their lives had ended. I assured my sister that I was going to build a house and buy her a car. I told her I would send her money to start her own business so that her boss, who had been transferring her to remote villages to work because she was not educated, would one day see her shine.

I left Cameroon without a dollar in my pocket, but God was faithful. Upon my arrival at the Dallas airport, I was paid fifty dollars for my bag that had been damaged. My sister, whom we call General Alice, hosted a big welcome party in my honor. The reception was majestic, and a great many people came to welcome me. One of the attendees was a woman with a cast on her leg; she had fallen and fractured it. Not knowing who this woman was, I asked her if I could pray for her. She nodded her head in approval, so I laid my hands on her and prayed. In less than twenty-four hours, she was miraculously healed by the power of God. This woman then called my sister-in-law, Mrs. Brenda Ngwa, and testified to her.

Needless to say, my sister who was hosting the reception was embarrassed by my actions because the woman I prayed for was a very important person.

After everyone had left that evening, my sister came to my room and said, "Bridget, listen to me carefully. This is America. Stop praying like you did in Africa. Also, in America nobody pays school fees for another; you will have to get a job and pay for your tuition."

"Sister, I replied, "the same God I served in Africa is the same God in America." I knew that with the comfort level found in America, I needed to pray even more than before, lest I grow lukewarm. In fact, the Lord had instructed me to enter America with a fast of 130 days, which I did. Prior to my arrival, I had also believed that everybody in America was godly, but I was wrong. I had seen so many godly missionaries from America back home in Cameroon that I thought all Americans were like that.

One of these missionaries, an elderly lady, died in Cameroon, and as I carried the reef of her burial, I tearfully prayed, "Lord, take me one day to her country to show the same love to her people that she showed to us." God answered that prayer when I was admitted into the American Indian College in Phoenix, Arizona. Even more amazing, one day I visited a church called

Sweet Water of the Valley. There I met the missionary's sister and pastor. God is all-knowing and so great!

As the only foreigner from Africa at American Indian College, I was loved by all, but I was lonesome for home and African food. I was still wearing braids as I had been accustomed to in Africa, so the students contributed money for me to change my hairstyle. My financial condition was so dire that I had to cut my own hair. Nevertheless, the staff and students of AIC treated me like family.

One night, I was suffering from a malarial fever, and the students thought that it was contagious. They became convinced that they too were feeling bad until the president's wife, Reverend (Mrs.) Collins explained my condition to them. She and her husband had been missionaries in Africa for over ten years and understood the way malaria worked.

God, through some members of First Assembly of God Church in Louisiana, helped me pay my tuition. However, during my second semester, I attended classes for over a month without payment. I was informed that if I did not pay one-third of my tuition by Friday, I would have to leave the campus.

On that Friday morning, I managed to get a few coins together to make a phone call to my elder sister. I asked her to assist me, but she replied, "If you quit school and promise to study pharmacy or become a medical doctor, I will pay your tuition for that. If you are determined to study and preach and do all those conferences, then I will not be a part of it." At the end of this conversation, my eyes were so filled with tears that I could hardly see, even though it was daylight. I forced myself to sing my song of encouragement:

I have decided to follow Jesus.
I have decided to follow Jesus.
I have decided to follow Jesus.
No turning back,
No turning back.

I sang this song loudly as I headed back to my room, each step seemingly taking me to nowhere. As I walked back to pack my belongings, hot tears streamed down my cheeks, and I longed for the rapture to take place. Of course, it did not. I wanted the world to end, but it did not.

I knelt down by my bed to say my last prayer at school. It was a lamentation of confused quarreling with God, a myriad of thoughts racing through my mind. *Why was I born into such a poor family?* I wondered. *Why should I be thrown out of school because I cannot afford fifteen hundred dollars? What can I do to end this cycle of affliction? I must get a college degree!* For three to four hours, I wept and lamented. Finally, I gathered enough courage to finish packing; then I sat on the bed, waiting for my roommate so that I could tell her good-bye.

Suddenly there was a knock on the door. "Are you in there?" came a voice.

I replied affirmatively, and then the voice said, "You are needed in the registration office." I wondered what was going on. Had there been a change of mind?

I walked into the office and saw a tall man standing there. The registrar said, "Meet Pastor Victor. He has just paid your tuition and given his credit card number for the balance. Do you know him?" I said no. "Have you ever seen him?" I said no. "Then this must be a true miracle!"

I thanked Pastor Victor with tears of great joy. "Who are you?" I asked. "Are you an angel sent by God? How did you know I was here?"

"Sister Mary told me about your ordeal, so I came to help," he responded. "God bless you," he added.

This was indeed a miracle, just like when I had been cold a few weeks earlier and God had sent two women to buy winter coats and blankets for me. Father God is always on time! That day I fell on my knees and began to praise God. He is so faithful. He is indeed a covenant-keeping God. He has promised to be with me always, and though I have failed Him many times, He has never failed me even once.

Pastors John and Bridget Israel

Chapter 8

God's Grace Is Sufficient

The grace of God successfully brought me through that school year. In my junior year, I was sent to Louisiana to participate in a summer internship. In the beginning, it was a great blessing. My testimony was broadcast on various television channels, and soon other television stations wanted to interview me.

For all the TV shows, I needed a black makeup artist and hair stylist, so I was taken to the south side of the city and introduced as a princess from Africa. My host left me there, since it was going to take the stylist at least two or three hours to do my hair. Once she departed, the stylist asked, "Are you really a princess?"

"Yes," I answered with a smile, not realizing the motive behind her question.

To my surprise, she continued with, "It was your fathers who sold us into slavery. You have a black president, and we will never have one. In all my life, I have never seen a black man in the White House."

With tears in my eyes, I replied, "I am sorry for what our ancestors did, but not for what my father did, because he fought against slavery. I pray that you will not die until a black man is President of the United States of America." Praise God, on November 4, 2008, President Barack Obama was elected as the Forty-fourth President of the United States. I remember that we declared a twenty-four-hour prayer chain for him. God still answers prayers! That hairstylist later became my good friend.

The television interviews went well. The whole state watched, and a group of inner-city children, mostly African Americans, saw the interviews. I was so excited when I was told that the children would like me to speak to them in person. So I directed her to the host, who approved it. It was scheduled for two weeks later.

A few days before I was to speak to the inner-city group, however, I was told not to go. When I asked why, I was told that a bigger and richer church wanted me on the same day, and the inner-city group was composed of poor blacks who had no money to support me. "Well, ma'am," I responded, "I am very sorry to disappoint you, but I am going to speak to the poor group. Look at me, when you say they are black. I am black too, and they are my brothers and sisters. My anointing is not for sale, but for whomever God has called me to reach. God loves all races and cannot be a racist."

She sternly warned, "They do not have money to support you. If you go to them, then let them file for you. All of the money raised to support you will be confiscated."

"No problem, ma'am," I calmly answered. "The God who has helped me will still be God. He has not run out of resources or people to use. Nobody is indispensable."

After that I did not go to school for some time because I had no money, but I was happy that I had stood my ground for the right thing. God eventually supernaturally helped me to graduate with a Bachelor of Arts degree in Education. I was the first in my family to earn a college degree. I was also certified as a teacher in Phoenix, Arizona, and I was offered a job in the school where I did my practical.

In order to accept this position, I had to obtain a work permit. While I was waiting for its release, God sent Prophetess Lucy to drive twenty-three hours to come and tell me to go into full-time ministry instead. I was very angry and shunned her for a week. But when we went for our Saturday morning Bible study, the same message was given to me by a different person. I relented and decided to obey the voice of the Lord.

On the following Monday, I handed in my badge and turned down the job offer. On my return home, I stopped at the mailbox to check my mail, only to find my work permit had come in that morning. I was tempted to call the principal; she reminded me that it is better to obey the voice of God. I then made my preparations and got rid of everything I owned. I gave my car to a single mom who had lost everything in a bitter divorce. All I had left were seven dresses, and I packed them in a suitcase and bought a one-way ticket to Los Angeles.

I was headed for the Dream Center, a church run by Pastor Matthew Barnett, whose father, Tommy Barnett, was my pastor in Phoenix, Arizona.

I also started a fast. For sixty-three days, I only drank liquids. When I arrived in Los Angeles, I was given a bed among all types of women. Some of them were on drugs, and some were former prostitutes or abused wives, but I saw it as the greatest ministry opportunity. We went to Hollywood Boulevard every evening to minister. I was having a great time.

On the sixty-second day of my fast, I heard a voice within that said: "You have not arrived at your destination. Expect a phone call and an air ticket for where I am sending you to start a new work. My church has been very busy with other programs and has neglected the master key of prayer. I am anointing you to carry the prayer power back to My church. Raise up intercessors and disciples to carry out My mission as stated in My Word: 'But upon Mount Zion shall be deliverance, and there shall be holiness; and the house of Jacob shall possess their possessions.' Put intercessors in every family. I am the Lord that answereth prayer. Abide in Me, and I will abide in you. I will never leave you nor forsake you. I am going to raise the financial pillars for My mission. Just obey Me, and all will be well with you."

I moved to Houston, Texas, where I had brethren in Christ waiting for me. The late Sister Helen Azaah, who had been my spiritual daughter before we came to America, hosted me in her apartment during our first meeting, and I washed the feet of everyone present. By the following Thursday, Sister Ukraie had given us the use of her banquet hall, called Victory Hall, for a few months. Elder Cyril and Deaconess Regine loaned us their office space for Bible study.

The good Lord who fulfills His promises began to multiply us through miracles, signs, and wonders. The place was soon too small to contain the crowd, so the church moved to a shopping plaza and rented space for about ten years. In this rented space, I made my home for a while.

I slept on a cardboard box as my bed. I could not cook because I had nowhere to cook, no pots, and no food to cook. I had no place to take a shower. There was no warm water or heater in the facility, and it was wintertime. Even though it did not snow in Houston, it was still very cold. I almost caught pneumonia because of bathing in cold water and sleeping in the cold.

Despite all the physical hardship I suffered, many people came for prayer. I would pray for them, and God would answer with signs, miracles, and wonders. The news of the Holy Spirit's power at work spread so fast that people were soon coming from all over. One family from Louisiana even flew their daughter in to receive deliverance prayer.

God was blessing many people through me, yet I was homeless. Many bought cars and houses, and I would rejoice and thank God with them, but I had nothing. In fact, my condition was so bad that a little boy called Poku came to see me one day with his mother (who is now Pastor Blessing) and compassionately offered me his one dollar so I could buy food and a house. Though his mother laughed, his kind gesture was an encouragement to me. I took it as a sign that one day I would own a house where I could take a warm bath.

I kept praying and preaching the Word of God. One day I heard in my spirit, "Go look for an apartment, for your time to be blessed has come." I immediately responded and was given a two-bedroom apartment to use free of charge for two weeks. I had no credit or salary, but when I shared my story with the landlady, she showed me kindness. God is faithful.

Now I had an apartment. Even though I had no furniture, I could at least take a warm bath or shower. My first bath was as exhilarating as taking a trip to Paris. I was so grateful for the simple pleasure that I felt as if I had won a million-dollar lottery. Sometimes, however, we can take things like a bed, a warm shower, or even clean water for granted. I slept on the floor for about a month until someone donated a twin-sized mattress. I felt as if I were living in a palace.

One thing is sure: God is who He says He is. He kept on blessing the ministry, and signs and wonders were taking place. People were being blessed, so they began to bless me in turn. They began to pay my rent on time, so I built up some credit.

A day came when I heard in my spirit to go and look for a house. I obeyed, but I had no down payment. I found a house that I liked, but to purchase it would require ten thousand dollars for the down payment. Ron, the sales agent, checked my credit and income and said that I would not qualify for the house. I merely looked at him and asked if he believed in miracles. I told him that he was going to see one, because I was going to buy that house. I then went to church and prayed and started fasting for God to make a way for me to get this house.

I traveled as usual to preach in Atlanta. The Lord performed signs and wonders, and one lady came to me and said that the Lord had instructed her to give me ten thousand dollars as a down payment for my house. It felt so unreal, as if I were dreaming. Tears of joy began streaming down my cheeks, and the woman, not knowing that she was an answer to prayer, became alarmed. All I could say was, "God bless you. Thank you very much. God bless you beyond your imagination. Thank you so very much."

By this time, my daughter, whom I had left in Africa at four years of age, was about ten years old. I thank my sister Ma Mary, who became both her mother and father. Miracle's father did not care about her, but God in His mercy provided for her. Through the help of a precious sister, Judge Helen, Miracle was admitted into secondary school. She graduated and received a General Certificate of Education (GCE).

Bear in mind that once upon a time, I was a woman insulted by my in-laws because I was barren. But God's blessings make rich and add no sorrow (Proverbs 10:22), and He eventually gifted me with my wonderful daughter. She finally joined me in America and is now the current Miss Cameroon USA and a student in a university.

At one point, a pastor warned a young girl who was following me and praying with me that I was a single woman and that she would not marry if she continued to follow me. But with deep groanings, I prayed to God for a husband for her: "Oh Lord, roll away this reproach, and please give this woman a husband so that this man will know that I serve the Living God." Within three months, God answered the prayer, and the young woman was married. On her wedding day, this pastor would not allow me to stand on his stage and bless the couple; I had to remain on the floor. Sadly, he looked down on me because I was single, but God saw that he despised me and intervened.

Another woman remarked to a sister that the day Pastor Bridget got married, she would come to church. I became a laughingstock to others, so sure they were that I would never marry. But God chose to honor His name in my life. Through Bishop Nkechi, who came to preach at Zion Covenant Ministries (also known as Zion House of Prayer), I was introduced to her senior pastor in London, England, Pastor John Israel. He called me, but in my heart, I did not want to marry a pastor. I wanted to marry a Christian businessman who would help by supporting me financially in my humanitarian works to build schools, hospitals, and homes for the less privileged. I wanted to continue from where Mother Teresa had stopped. I did not want any child to suffer what I had suffered, especially the lack of basic necessities like food, water, clothes, or shelter. I wanted to help poor farmers' children to achieve quality education. I still believe that not long from now, God will make me a blessing to many as He grants me the grace.

Anyway, I did not initially like Pastor John Israel. I started ignoring his calls, so he finally gave up his pursuit of me. However, Bishop Nkechi pressured him to call again. One day my phone rang, and I answered it, thinking the call was from a business friend in China. It was Pastor John. He and I reconnected, and he then flew to America to see me.

When I met him at the airport, he was wearing a big diamond cross on a chain around his neck, which turned me off. I had also assumed he would dress up in an effort to impress me, but he had not. But God, who is all-knowing, later convicted me of my prejudice.

Leaving the airport, I asked Pastor John if we could stop at a restaurant to get something to eat, because I did not cook. He said he wanted to meet my mother first. We talked about other things until we drew near my favorite restaurant. I asked again if we could stop to get something to eat, but he raised his voice and insisted on seeing my mother first. At this point, I was completely turned off. I wished that he would catch the next available flight back to London, but I had to fake being nice, for Christ's sake.

Finally we arrived at my house, and my mother opened the door. The way Pastor John greeted her captivated her heart. She later asked me who he was, and I told her that he was a pastor who had come to preach. I had hosted many pastors, so this was not a new thing to my mother. She said that he greeted her like a son, and she liked him. In my mind, I wished she knew how I felt about him.

It was a Thursday, and I had a miracle service to conduct. I left Pastor John with my mother, not even caring what he would eat or what my mother would cook. Later he came to the church, and I introduced him. Taking the microphone, he sang two songs, and the church went wild. We were all taken aback by the anointed energy that emanated from his worship. Some people were weeping, and others were on their knees, worshiping God. The service lasted until 10:00 p.m., and no one left early. In fact, we all wanted more.

The Friday that followed was our Holy Ghost night vigil. Pastor John sang and preached and prayed until 4:00 a.m. People were so blessed that they requested his return. Even with all this enthusiasm and acceptance of him, my mind was still not made up about him. As soon as he left, however, two elderly sisters approached me and said they had been praying for a husband for me and that Pastor John was the man. I smiled and politely told them I would pray about it.

It had been some time since my spiritual father, Prophet Kure Emmanuel, had come to speak at our Fire Conference. When I saw him again and gave him the names of all the men who were asking for my hand in marriage, he rejected all of them. I then jokingly told him about Pastor John, and he called him to arrange for a visit. Before the prophet told me that Pastor John was to be my husband, another man, Dr. Chris Wilmot, saw him in the prophet's suit and said that he was to be my husband. I had been disappointed before, so I had to know for myself.

One day I went to help a man of God called Captain Chibo. Without my telling him anything, he said that God had sent a young man to help me in ministry, but I was thinking of putting him away. He told me not to do it. He said that this man was a blessing from God for both me and my ministry.

He was right on target with his words. Pastor John had indeed offended me again, and I had planned to end it after he finished preaching. I did not want my words to affect his spirit beforehand, so I had not yet told him anything. However, God again outsmarted me and sent Captain Chibo to speak to me.

How long would I keep running? I decided to ask Pastor John what his vision was. When he told me, my heart jumped in excitement. He soon asked me to marry him, and I said that he would have to ask me this question before the congregation. He had returned to London by this time, but he agreed to come back. In my heart, however, I was still dragging my feet.

As I left for the airport to pick him up, I asked the Lord to please help me to get to the airport before Pastor John came through security. Every other time he had come, I had made him wait for me. But I got lost on my way to the airport, and I did not get there until 4:00 p.m. Though his flight had been scheduled to arrive between 2:00 and 2:30 p.m., he had not yet come through security when I arrived.

I smiled broadly when I saw him and asked what had happened. He explained how the flight had landed but the door of the plane would not open for a while. I knew that this was the answer to my prayer. God, by His invisible but invincible, mighty hand, held that door closed until I arrived. What a mighty God we serve!

On the twenty-third of December, Pastor John Israel and I became engaged at Zion Covenant Ministries. The last thing that really sealed the deal for me was the gift he gave me on Christmas. I had seen a certain diamond chain advertised on television that I wished I could have, and he gave me that very chain. To make things even more interesting, I learned that we shared the same birthday. Thus we decided to wed on our birthday, and it came to pass.

Our wedding made history in the Christian community. Prophet Kure officiated the wedding. God blessed the people who sponsored the wedding in such a grand way. It was like Eddie Murphy's *Coming to America* film. But you don't have to take my word for it. Come to Zion Covenant Ministries and see the pictures for yourself. See how mighty men of valor carried me into the reception hall on that glorious day. Indeed God has turned my scars into stars!

The same God who has changed my story will do the same and more for you if you will call upon Him in truth. Remember, there is hope for you. No condition is permanent. Have faith in God without ceasing. If you can pray, God can answer, for prayer connects the visible with the invisible.

If you need prayer, do not hesitate to e-mail me at bfominyam@yahoo.com, or call 281-575-7700. May God bless you and all your loved ones.

Remember in the desert you saw how the Lord your God carried you, like one carries a child. And He has brought you safely all the way to this place.
— Deuteronomy 1:31

But upon Mount Zion shall be deliverance, and there shall be holiness; and the house of Jacob shall possess their possessions.
—Obadiah 1:17

Decision Page

I invite you to make Jesus Christ your Lord and Savior, if you have never done so. Boycott hell and embrace eternal life through believing in Jesus as your personal and only Savior. Prayer will not work if you do not belong to the Kingdom of God. With sincerity of heart, you must declare for Jesus. If you would like to make Jesus your Lord and Savior, please pray the following prayer from your heart:

Dear Jesus, I believe You died for me and that You rose again on the third day. I confess to You that I am a sinner and that I need Your love and forgiveness. Come into my life today, and forgive my sins and turn my life around. With my mouth, I confess that You are the Son of God. In my heart, I believe that God raised

You from the dead. I declare that You are my Savior, Lord, and Master.

Thank You, Lord Jesus, for saving me. From today forward, help me to walk in Your peace, love, forgiveness, and joy. Give me Your Holy Spirit to teach me, guide me, and order my steps in Your Word. In Jesus' name I pray. I am now born again—hallelujah!

Signed _____   Date: _____

Call somebody to testify of your salvation, because choosing Jesus Christ is the best choice you can ever make!

For counseling, ministry, or conference requests, contact me at:

281-575-7700

Website: http://www.zionbreadoflife.org

E-mail: bfominyam@yahoo.com

Or write to:

Zion Covenant Ministries

2340 Barker Oaks Drive

Houston, Texas 77077

CPSIA information can be obtained
at www.ICGtesting.com
Printed in the USA
FFOW03n1805140218
45093008-45518FF